Copyright © 2024 Celai West

All right reserved.

No part of this book may be reproduced, or stored in any retrieval system, or transmitted in any form or by any means, electronic, mechanical, photocopying, recording, or otherwise, without express written permission of the publisher.

PREFACE

---※---

I created this journal because I noticed I began falling down the rabbit hole of negative self-talk and I know I'm not the only teen experiencing this. My goal with this journal is for you to realize the power of your words, both good and bad, while offering you the tools to challenge and overcome negative thoughts. Each page is filled with prompts and exercises crafted to boost your self-esteem, promote positive thinking and improve teen mental health. These activities help shift your focus from what's going wrong to what's going right. Whether you're battling stress from school, friendships, or just life in general, this journal is here to remind you that you're capable of greatness.

My journal incorporates techniques I personally use to help me to manage stress, build resilience, and cultivate a positive outlook on life! Watch how your mindset transforms over time with weekly check-ins and goal-setting sections. Celebrate your wins, big and small!

BENEFITS OF USING THE TEEN SURVIVAL GUIDE:

- **Boosts Self-Esteem:** Regular journaling helps you focus on your positive qualities and achievements, building your confidence.
- **Reduces Stress:** Writing about your thoughts and feelings can be a great way to release stress and anxiety.
- **Encourages Mindfulness:** Our prompts encourage you to be present and mindful, helping you to appreciate the moment and reduce negative self-talk.
- **Enhances Emotional Intelligence:** By reflecting on your emotions, you'll gain a better understanding of yourself and others.

Don't let negative self-talk hold you back. Take the first step towards a happier, more confident you with the Teen Survival Guide. Embrace your power, rewrite your story, and watch your world change for the better.

Talk a little nicer to yourself today...

TODAY'S DATE: _____

I'M VERY GOOD AT:

_____
_____
_____
_____
_____
_____
_____
_____
_____
_____
_____
_____
_____
_____
_____

HOW DID I DISCOVER I WAS VERY GOOD AT THIS:

_____
_____
_____
_____

TODAY'S DATE: _____

THINGS I DO BETTER THAN MOST PEOPLE:

_____
_____
_____
_____
_____
_____
_____
_____
_____
_____
_____
_____
_____
_____
_____
_____
_____
_____

HOW & WHEN DID I DISCOVER THIS:

_____
_____
_____
_____
_____

Date: _____

FEELINGS AND EMOTIONS

 ANGRY

1. What things make me feel this way?
_____
_____
_____

2. What thoughts do I have when you feel like this?
_____
_____
_____

3. What <u>negative</u> things do I tell myself when I feel angry?
_____
_____
_____

4. What coping skills can I use to better deal with this emotion?
_____
_____
_____

5. What <u>positive</u> things can I tell myself when I start feeling angry?
_____
_____
_____

FEELINGS CHECK-IN

Right now, I'm feeling...

I feel this way because:

_____
_____
_____
_____

Something that might help is:

WEEKLY CHECK-IN

Date: _____

S M T W T F S

PRIORITIES

....
....
....

TO DO LIST

☐ ....
☐ ....
☐ ....
☐ ....
☐ ....

GOALS

....

NOTES

....
....
....

TALK TO YOURSELF LIKE YOU WOULD TALK TO SOMEONE YOU LOVE.

TODAY'S DATE: _____

WHAT IS SOMETHING PEOPLE COMPLIMENT ME THE MOST ABOUT:
_____
_____
_____

WHAT ARE MY THOUGHTS/FEELINGS ABOUT THIS:
_____
_____

WHAT IS MY BIGGEST ACCOMPLISHMENT:
_____
_____
_____

HOW DOES IT MAKE ME FEEL?
_____
_____

WHAT DID I ENJOY DOING THE MOST AS A YOUNG CHILD:
_____
_____
_____
_____
_____

TODAY'S DATE: _____

MY FAVORITE FACIAL FEATURE(S):
_____
_____

WHY?
_____
_____

MY FAVORITE BODY PART(S):
_____
_____

WHY?
_____
_____

MY FAVORITE PERSONALITY TRAIT(S):
_____
_____

WHY?
_____
_____

I am...

F	P	A	T	I	E	N	T	H	N	H	G
P	O	S	I	T	I	V	E	A	D	W	I
A	T	A	L	E	N	T	E	D	P	O	F
B	R	A	V	E	N	O	U	G	H	R	T
B	W	O	N	D	E	R	F	U	L	T	E
S	T	R	O	N	G	K	I	N	D	H	D
A	G	C	A	R	I	N	G	G	C	Y	V
W	Y	B	E	A	U	T	I	F	U	L	M

Find as many words that describe you.

FEELINGS CHECK-IN

Right now, I'm feeling...

I feel this way because:
_____
_____
_____
_____

Something that might help is:

WEEKLY CHECK-IN

Date: _____

S M T W T F S

TO DO LIST

- ☐ ....
- ☐ ....
- ☐ ....
- ☐ ....
- ☐ ....

PRIORITIES

....
....
....

GOALS

....
....

NOTES

....
....
....

TODAY'S DATE: _____

HOW DO I TALK TO MYSELF WHEN I AM FEELING INSECURE:
_____
_____
_____
_____
_____
_____
_____
_____
_____
_____
_____
_____

I CAN CHANGE THIS BY...
_____
_____
_____
_____
_____
_____
_____

TODAY'S DATE: _____

WHAT ARE MY GREATEST STRENGTHS:

_____
_____
_____
_____
_____
_____
_____
_____
_____
_____

WHAT ARE MY GREATEST WEAKNESSES:

_____
_____
_____
_____
_____
_____
_____
_____
_____
_____

FEELINGS AND EMOTIONS
WORRIED

1. What things make me feel this way?
   _____
   _____
   _____

2. What thoughts do I have when I feel like this?
   _____
   _____
   _____

3. What <u>negative</u> things do I tell yourself when I feel worried?
   _____
   _____
   _____

4. What coping skills can I use to better deal with this emotion?
   _____
   _____
   _____

5. What <u>positive</u> things can I tell myself when I start feeling worried?
   _____
   _____
   _____

FEELINGS CHECK-IN

Right now, I'm feeling...

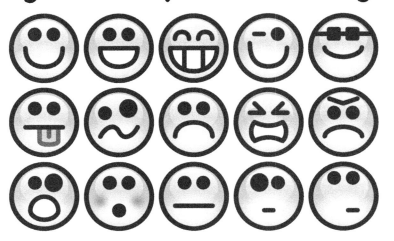

I feel this way because:

_____

_____

_____

_____

Positive words that might help me:

WEEKLY CHECK-IN

Date: ....

S M T W T F S

TO DO LIST

PRIORITIES

GOALS

NOTES

> THE WORDS YOU TELL YOURSELF MATTER. THEY CAN EITHER LIFT YOU UP OR TEAR YOU DOWN
>
> *choose them wisely*

TODAY'S DATE: _____

WHAT PERSONAL QUALITIES DO I WANT TO DEVELOP:
_____
_____
_____
_____
_____
_____
_____
_____
_____
_____

WHAT DO I WANT TO ELIMINATE FROM MY LIFE:
_____
_____
_____
_____
_____
_____
_____
_____
_____
_____

TODAY'S DATE: _____

HOW CAN I BE MORE HONEST WITH MYSELF:

_____
_____
_____
_____
_____
_____
_____
_____
_____
_____
_____
_____

WHAT'S MOST IMPORTANT TO ME RIGHT NOW:

_____
_____
_____
_____
_____
_____
_____
_____
_____
_____
_____
_____

When I feel upset, these 5 things make me feel better:

1. _____
2. _____
3. _____
4. _____
5. _____

When I feel upset, these 5 things make me feel worse:

1. _____
2. _____
3. _____
4. _____
5. _____

FEELINGS CHECK-IN

Right now, I'm feeling...

I feel this way because:

Activities that might help me:

WHEN THINGS CHANGE INSIDE YOU, things CHANGE AROUND you

TODAY'S DATE: _____

HOW DO I TALK TO MYSELF WHEN I AM FEELING INVISIBLE:

_____
_____
_____
_____
_____
_____
_____
_____
_____
_____
_____
_____
_____
_____
_____

I CAN CHANGE THIS BY...

_____
_____
_____
_____
_____
_____
_____

TODAY'S DATE: _____

SOMETHING(S) I WISH MORE PEOPLE KNEW ABOUT ME:

_____
_____
_____
_____
_____
_____
_____
_____
_____
_____
_____
_____

SOMETHING(S) I WISH NOBODY KNEW ABOUT ME:

_____
_____
_____
_____
_____
_____
_____
_____
_____
_____
_____
_____

Date: _____

FEELINGS AND EMOTIONS

SAD

1. What things make me feel this way?
_____
_____
_____

2. What thoughts do I have when I feel like this?
_____
_____
_____

3. What <u>negative</u> things do I tell myself when I feel sad?
_____
_____
_____

4. What coping skills can I use to better deal with this emotion?
_____
_____
_____

5. What <u>positive</u> things can I tell myself when I start feeling sad?
_____
_____
_____

FEELINGS CHECK-IN

Right now, I'm feeling...

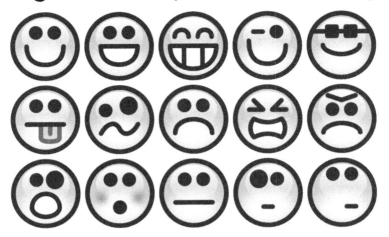

I feel this way because:

_____
_____
_____
_____

Positive words that might help me:

WEEKLY CHECK-IN

Date: _____

S M T W T F S

TO DO LIST
- ....
- ....
- ....
- ....
- ....

PRIORITIES
....
....
....

GOALS
....
....

NOTES
....
....
....

BE CAREFUL HOW YOU TALK TO YOURSELF BECAUSE YOU ARE LISTENING

TODAY'S DATE: _____

HOW DO I TALK TO MYSELF WHEN I AM FEELING REJECTED:
_____
_____
_____
_____
_____
_____
_____
_____
_____
_____
_____
_____
_____
_____
_____
_____

I CAN CHANGE THIS BY...
_____
_____
_____
_____
_____
_____
_____

TODAY'S DATE: _____

WHAT INSPIRES & MOTIVATES ME THE MOST:

_____
_____
_____
_____
_____
_____
_____
_____
_____
_____
_____
_____
_____

HOW CAN I FIND MORE WAYS TO DO THESE THINGS MORE OFTEN:

_____
_____
_____
_____
_____
_____
_____

MAZE FUN

FEELINGS CHECK-IN

Right now, I'm feeling...

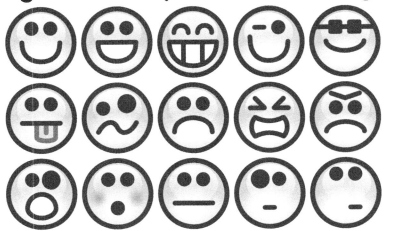

I feel this way because:

_____
_____
_____
_____

Activities that might help me:

Things To Give Up

- [ ] 1. Negative thinking
- [ ] 2. Doubting myself
- [ ] 3. Negative self-talk
- [ ] 4. Fear of failure
- [ ] 5. Criticizing others
- [ ] 6. Fear of success
- [ ] 7. People pleasing
- [ ] 8. Procrastination

TODAY'S DATE: _____

WHAT ARE MY WEAKNESSES:
_____
_____
_____
_____
_____
_____

HOW DID I DISCOVER THIS:
_____
_____
_____
_____
_____
_____

WHAT PROBLEMS COULD THIS CAUSE:
_____
_____
_____
_____
_____
_____
_____
_____
_____

TODAY'S DATE: _____

WHAT ACTIVITIES DO I DISLIKE DOING:
_____
_____
_____
_____
_____
_____
_____
_____

WHY?
_____
_____
_____
_____
_____
_____
_____

HOW CAN I MAKE IT MORE ENJOYABLE:
_____
_____
_____
_____
_____
_____
_____

Date: _____

FEELINGS AND EMOTIONS
EMBARRASSED

1. What things make me feel this way?
_____
_____
_____

2. What thoughts do I have when I feel like this?
_____
_____
_____

3. What <u>negative</u> things do I tell myself when I feel embarrassed?
_____
_____
_____

4. What coping skills can I use to better deal with this emotion?
_____
_____
_____

5. What <u>positive</u> things can I tell myself when I start feeling embarrassed?
_____
_____
_____

FEELINGS CHECK-IN

Right now, I'm feeling...

I feel this way because:
_____
_____
_____
_____

Encouraging words that might help me:

WEEKLY CHECK-IN

Date: _____

S M T W T F S

TO DO LIST
- ☐ ....
- ☐ ....
- ☐ ....
- ☐ ....
- ☐ ....

PRIORITIES
....
....
....

GOALS
....
....

NOTES
....
....
....

- I have the power to control my thoughts.
- Less self-judgement and more self-love.
- I am confident I can achieve any goal.
- I am strong, brave and resilient.
- **POSITIVE THINK**
- I am at peace with my past.
- I choose happiness everyday.
- I am not afraid to be myself.
- I am letting go of what no longer serves me.

TODAY'S DATE: _____

WHAT PARTS OF MY PERSONALITY ARE HOLDING ME BACK:
_____
_____
_____
_____
_____
_____
_____

HOW?
_____
_____
_____
_____
_____
_____
_____

HOW CAN I CHANGE THIS:
_____
_____
_____
_____
_____
_____

TODAY'S DATE: _____

WHAT DO I CARE ABOUT THE MOST:
_____
_____
_____
_____
_____
_____
_____
_____

WHY?
_____
_____
_____
_____
_____
_____
_____
_____

HOW DOES IT MAKE ME FEEL:
_____
_____
_____
_____
_____
_____

FEELINGS AND EMOTIONS

 SCARED

1. What things make me feel this way?
_____
_____
_____

2. What thoughts do I have when I feel like this?
_____
_____
_____

3. What <u>negative</u> things do I tell myself when I feel scared?
_____
_____
_____

4. What coping skills can I use to better deal with this emotion?
_____
_____
_____

5. What <u>positive</u> things can I tell myself when I start feeling scared?
_____
_____
_____

FEELINGS CHECK-IN

Right now, I'm feeling...

I feel this way because:
_____
_____
_____
_____

Motivating words that might help me:

WEEKLY CHECK-IN

Date: _____

S M T W T F S

TO DO LIST

PRIORITIES

GOALS

NOTES

NOTE TO SELF

I AM

- ☑ AMAZING
- ☑ BRAVE
- ☑ BEAUTIFUL
- ☑ CONFIDENT
- ☑ STRONG

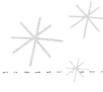

TODAY'S DATE: _____

WHO IS THE MOST POSITIVE/SUPPORTIVE PERSON I KNOW:
_____
_____
_____
_____
_____

A TIME I FELT REALLY DISCOURAGED AND THEY HELPED ME WAS WHEN...
_____
_____
_____
_____
_____
_____
_____
_____
_____
_____
_____
_____
_____
_____
_____
_____
_____

TODAY'S DATE: _____

WHAT PART(S) OF MY LIFE DRAIN MY ENERGY THE MOST:
_____
_____
_____
_____
_____
_____
_____
_____
_____
_____
_____
_____
_____
_____
_____
_____
_____

WHAT WOULD I DO TO CHANGE IT:
_____
_____
_____
_____
_____

TODAY'S DATE: _____

HOW WOULD I TALK TO MYSELF IF I WERE MORE CONFIDENT AND HAPPY:
_____
_____
_____
_____
_____
_____
_____
_____
_____
_____
_____
_____

WHAT AM I THE MOST PROUD OF:
_____
_____
_____
_____
_____
_____
_____
_____
_____
_____
_____

FEELINGS CHECK-IN

Right now, I'm feeling...

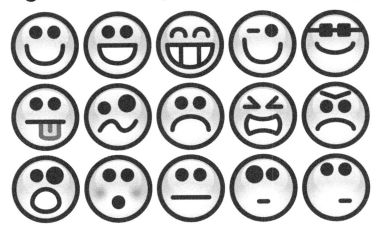

I feel this way because:
_____
_____
_____
_____

Something that might help is:

WEEKLY CHECK-IN

Date: _____

S M T W T F S

TO DO LIST

- ☐ ....
- ☐ ....
- ☐ ....
- ☐ ....
- ☐ ....

PRIORITIES

....
....
....

GOALS

....
....
....

NOTES

....
....
....

Be Positive checklist

- ◯ Is this worth getting upset over?

- ◯ Am I overreacting or over-thinking?

- ◯ What is the lesson or what can I learn from this?

- ◯ What is the positive takeaway from this?

- ◯ How is this making me a better person?

- ◯ Can I control this situation?

- ◯ What can I do to make myself feel better right now?

- ◯ How can I view this situation positively?

TODAY'S DATE: _____

WHAT IS MY FAVORITE SUBJECT IN SCHOOL AND WHY:
_____
_____
_____
_____
_____
_____
_____
_____
_____
_____
_____
_____
_____
_____
_____
_____

HOW/WHEN DID I DISCOVER I ENJOYED THIS SUBJECT:
_____
_____
_____
_____
_____

TODAY'S DATE: _____

I FEEL MOST UNMOTIVATED WHEN...

_____
_____
_____
_____
_____
_____
_____
_____
_____
_____
_____
_____
_____
_____
_____

I CAN CHANGE THIS BY...

_____
_____
_____
_____
_____
_____
_____

Feelings

Draw, write or describe what can help you when you are feeling each of these emotions.

When I feel disappointed...

When I need a break...

When I feel powerless...

When I feel lonely...

When I feel jealous...

FEELINGS CHECK-IN

Right now, I'm feeling...

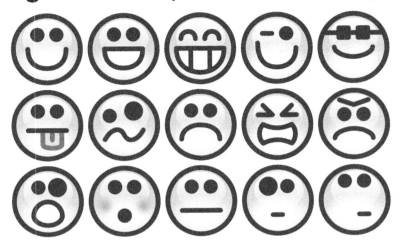

I feel this way because:

_____
_____
_____
_____

Something that might help is:

WEEKLY CHECK-IN

Date: _____

S M T W T F S

TO DO LIST

PRIORITIES

GOALS

NOTES

MY NOTES

MY NOTES

MY NOTES

MY NOTES

MY NOTES

MY NOTES

MY NOTES

MY NOTES

MY NOTES

MY NOTES

MY NOTES

MY NOTES

MY NOTES

MY NOTES

MY NOTES

MY NOTES

MY NOTES

MY NOTES

MY NOTES

MY NOTES

RANDOM THOUGHTS

RANDOM THOUGHTS

RANDOM THOUGHTS

RANDOM THOUGHTS

RANDOM THOUGHTS

RANDOM THOUGHTS

RANDOM THOUGHTS

RANDOM THOUGHTS

RANDOM THOUGHTS

RANDOM THOUGHTS

MY FEELINGS

MY FEELINGS

MY FEELINGS

MY FEELINGS

MY FEELINGS

MY FEELINGS

MY FEELINGS

MY FEELINGS

MY FEELINGS

MY FEELINGS

Made in the USA
Middletown, DE
04 May 2025

75115182R00071